# Inspirational Resources
# for Women's Groups

# Inspirational Resources for Women's Groups

**Helen Lowrie Marshall**

**BAKER BOOK HOUSE**
Grand Rapids, Michigan 49506

ISBN: 0-8010-6196-2

Printed in the United States of America

These poems by Helen Lowrie Marshall were
selected from her popular books: *Starlight
and Candleglow, Leave a Touch of Glory, Quiet
Power, The Gift of Wonder, Walk the World
Proudly, Bright Horizons, Hold to Your Dream,
Aim for a Star, Dare to Be Happy, Close to the
Heart.*

# Contents

# Prayer at the New Year

At this, the time of high-borne resolutions,
We, too, would offer up this earnest prayer—
That we may know the priceless worth of friendships,
And keep those friendships always in repair;

That we may never take a love for granted,
Or lightly treat the thoughts of those who care,
But treasure every friendship's precious cargo—
And keep those friendships always in repair.

# Make a Joyful Noise

Make a joyful noise! The Good Book
  Says it many ways—
Serve with joy and gladness,
  Be generous with praise.

Wear a cheerful countenance,
  Rejoice in joy of others;
Let your speaking be with grace,
  Regard all men as brothers.

Love your neighbor as yourself,
  Speak evil of no one;
With dignity and pride go forth
  To meet each morning's sun.

Seek the true and beautiful,
  Let not your heart be sad;
Do good to them that hate you,
  Love the good, despise the bad.

Make a joyful noise, and sing
  A new song every day—
And may God's peace and joy and love
  Go with you all the way.

# New Mornings

New mornings—each a precious gift
  Alike to rich and poor,
Fresh with promise, bright with hope,
  Delivered at our door.

Tied with ribbons of the dawn
  To give the heart a lift,
Never two the same—each one
  A very special gift.

To be accepted graciously,
  As in the spirit given
By that Creator of all days;
  Delivered fresh from heaven.

New mornings—new beginnings—
  Alike for rich and poor,
A never-failing gift of hope
  Left daily at our door.

# More Time to Live

We ought to take more time to live—
  More time to really see
The glory and the wonders of this earth;
The quiet, gentle beauty,
  The sheer nobility
Revealed alone to those who prize its worth.

We ought to take more time to care—
  To really, truly care,
Enough to fling our heart's door open wide;
To lend a helping hand and share
  The burdens others bear,
And take the poor and comfortless inside.

We ought to take more time to feel—
  To surely, deeply feel
The quiet depth and power of God's love;
The close-enfolding presence of his peace,
  Profound and real,
The faith that lifts the soul to heights above.

We ought to take more time to live—
  To wholly, truly live,
More time to feel and care, more time to see;
To fully realize the endless joys
  That life can give,
To laugh—and love—and live abundantly!

# When and Where I Can

Dear God, please give to me to see
  The things that I can do
The ways that I can spend my time
  And self in serving you.

Let me accept the challenge
  Of those things within my power
To bring about a better world
  In this, my little hour.

And give me understanding, too,
  That I may know and see
What lies beyond the limits
  Of the powers given me.

Let me not be envious of those
  Who mountains move,
But let me wield my ounce of strength
  For you with grateful love.

Not holding back for those whose skill
  And talents mine outspan,
But with such gifts as may be mine
  Serve when and where I can.

# Whatever Your Gift

What is that you hold in your hand?
Nothing, you say? Look again.
Every hand holds some special gift—
A hammer, a broom, a pen,
A hoe, a scalpel, an artist's brush,
A needle, a microscope,
A violin's bow, a way with words
In the giving of faith and hope.
What is that you hold in your hand?
Whatever your gift may be,
It can open your door to abundant life—
You hold in your hand the key.

# What Can I Do?

What can I do—only one—
When such great tasks need to be done?
Right wrestles wrong upon the brink—
What can I do?
          I can think.

What can I do—only I?
War clouds hang heavy in the sky;
So grave the problems of today—
What can I do?
          I can pray.

What can I do—just one vote?
Can strength lie in so weak a note?
Yet—one voice shouting from the peak
Will carry far—
          And I can speak.

# Think and Be Glad

It's a busy world we live in,
  We get caught in the race,
And sometimes our sense of values
  Slips a little out of place.

It's a good thing to pull over
  To the roadside now and then
And get our thinking straightened out
  Before we start again.

And, like as not, we'll find a thought
  Or two to make us glad,
Some blessing that we've overlooked—
  Forgotten that we had.

A few good honest thoughts and
  Chances are that we'll arrive
At the heartening conclusion
  That it's good to be alive.

There's a new exciting challenge
  In the race of life when viewed
With a heart refreshed with gladness,
  And with prayerful gratitude.

# God Give Us Growth

God give us growth—a deeper joy in serving,
A fuller understanding of your will;
A firm and constant faith that knows no swerving,
The courage our commitments to fulfill.

Give us to grow in spiritual insight,
Make keener our awareness of the power
Of prayer to turn the darkness into daylight
And give us strength to meet each trying hour.

We would expand the compass of our thinking
To gather in its scope the whole world's need;
To recognize the Christian interlinking
Of every race and color, class and creed.

God give us growth—each day in all our living
That we may feel your presence over all,
Your blessing on each service—every giving.
God give us growth till we be heaven-tall.

# One Thing More

We may know love, respect, compassion, care,
But, lacking one more thing, our life is bare.
Unless we feel we're needed here on earth,
All else will be of very little worth.
Unless we have an opportunity
To live the Golden Rule, our life will be
An empty thing, unhappy at the core—
The human soul demands this one thing more.
We may know love, respect, compassion, care,
But let us have another's cross to share,
Another's burden we can help to pull—
Then, only, will our life be meaningful.

# Eyes of Understanding

Let me see life through a thousand eyes,
  The eyes of the young and old,
The tear-filled eyes and the laughing eyes,
  The eyes of the faint and bold.

Let me feel hurt as my neighbor feels,
  And thrill to his happiness;
Let me cringe at the blow the other one takes,
  Or glow with another's success.

Let me stand in the footsteps of every man
  Who travels on paths with me;
Let me understand him as only I can
  When I see what his own eyes see.

# A Candle of Understanding

There is so much darkness
  Encompassing about,
But deep within a candle waits
  To drive the darkness out.

The light of understanding
  Others' problems to perceive,
A gift that's freely given—
  Simply ask—you will receive.

A light of deeper insight
  Into problems others know—
A candle light to guide us
  In the way that we should go.

To do our part to bring about
  A time of peace on earth—
A light of understanding
  Of our own and others' worth.

# Power to Lift

If God has given you the special power
Of lightening another's shadowed hour;
If others turn to you for help in need,
Then is your life a blessed one, indeed.

But if, by grace divine, yours is the gift
To cheer men's lives—to comfort and to lift,
By that same token you have power, too,
To wound those others who look up to you.

However great our power to upraise
And change another's life by word of praise,
Just so great is our power to crush and bruise,
If we that special gift of God abuse.

So if the God of Love has chosen you
To trust his labors of compassion to,
Oh, take care lest you use his precious gift
To hurt those who look up to you to lift.

# How Good It Is

What a good thing it is that hope lives on
  Deep in our heart of hearts;
What a good thing it is to find ourselves
  Singing when music starts.

What a very good thing it is that when
  The Creator concocted man,
He threw in a dash of humor just
  To spice his practical plan.

How wonderful it is that love
  Can be the driving power
To shape and rule these lives of ours
  Through every waking hour.

What a glorious thing it is that men
  Are not like peas in a pod,
But each in his individual way
  The image of his God.

# The Commonplace

Thank the good Lord for the commonplace,
The thousand and one little ways
That lend a contentment and gladness and warmth
To all of our everydays.
Thank the great Giver of happy gifts—
Of sunshine and rain and snow,
Of flowers and books and families and friends
And every love we know.

# A Faith to Live By

Give me the faith of adventure, Lord,
  The courage to try the new,
The will to press on in spite of the dark,
  Knowing I walk with you.

Give me the faith of desire and hope,
  The inward urge to achieve.
All things are possible with you.
  O Lord, let me believe!

Give me the faith of awareness
  Of beauty everywhere,
Eyes to see, and ears to hear—
  An open heart to care.

Give me a faith to live by,
  Joyous and unafraid,
A glorious faith to match the dawn
  Of this day you have made!

# A Faith that Smiles

Give us a faith in the worth of ourselves,
And faith in our fellowman;
Give us a faith that right will prevail
In the infinite over-all plan;
Give us a faith in the future—
A farmer's faith in the sod,
A faith in eternal justice,
A faith in the love of God;
Give us a faith for the journey of life,
A strength for the winding miles,
A faith to sustain—but above all, Lord,
Give us a faith that smiles!

# A Faith that Holds

Dear God, give us a faith with holding power,
Not just a faith that blooms when life's a-flower,
Not just a faith that answers duty's call,
But faith that finds its way to cover all—
The sunny days that rouse a grateful heart,
The cloudy days, of every life a part,
The stark, black days when everything seems gone—
Dear God, give us a faith to carry on,
Our hand in yours with grasp so firm and tight
That it will hold through all—the wrong, the right—
Knowing that every day your love enfolds.
Dear God, give us, we pray, a faith that holds.

# Give Us This Day

God of forgotten ones everywhere,
Friend of the fatherless, hear our prayer—
We ask so little—not fame, nor wealth,
Nor even happiness, nor health.
We only ask that we be fed—
"Give us this day our daily bread."

Father of all the orphaned ones,
We, who were born to the sound of guns,
Upon whose shoulders, frail, must bear
The world's grim weight of want and care;
We pray now, as the Master said—
"Give us this day our daily bread."

God of the world, if you would touch
The hearts of those who have so much;
Help them to see the empty hands
Reaching to them from war-torn lands.
By your great mercy may they be led—
"Give us this day our daily bread."

# Beyond Measure

How can one measure friendship—
The firm, warm clasp of a hand,
The comfort found in the welcome sound
Of the words, "I understand"?

How can one measure courage—
The strength we find to fight,
To suffer life's anxieties,
To stand up for the right?

How can one measure beauty, hope,
Or happiness, or love?
What man-made measure can encompass
Faith in God above?

So much of life—the best of life—
The things we truly treasure,
Are these, the gifts of boundless depth
Beyond all earthly measure.

# Fellowship

Fellowship's a maker of friendships—
Think back on your life and see
How many friendships you can trace
To this spirit of harmony.

Fellowship—working with others
Has a way of bringing to light
Talents and gifts we might never know
With only a greeting polite.

Fellowship's more than the privilege
Of getting to know each other;
It's a Christian obligation
To join hands with your brother.

It's a Christian's obligation
To share in work to be done,
And the good Lord adds fellowship
To make the work seem more fun.

Yes, fellowship is God's own way
Of joining with labor and mirth
The hands and hearts of his people
In building his kingdom on earth.

# Did I Betray My Lord?

Did I betray my Lord today?
Dear God, could it be I?

Could he have been the beggar
On the street that I passed by?
Was his the silent call for help
I heard but did not heed?
Were his the hands that I ignored
Held out to me in need?
Were his the causes I declined
Because I had no time
To spare in helping rid his world
Of ignorance and crime?

I'd rather not become involved,
I'd my own life to live.
Others who liked that sort of thing
Had so much more to give.
There was not time enough, I said,
And begging should be barred.
Someone should see the poor were fed;
Why should my day be marred
By such unpleasant incidents?
And so I turned away.

Dear God, forgive me— it was I
Betrayed my Lord today.

# God Bring the Spring

God bring the spring to this old world,
　So bound with icy hate,
The warming sun of brotherhood,
　Its cold winds to abate.

God bring the miracle of spring,
　The promise of new life,
The fresh, still dews of quietness
　On bitterness and strife.

God plant the pulsing seeds of love
　Within the hearts of men
That they may end the winter's wars—
　God bring the spring again.

# Easter Prayer

We thank you for the joy that Easter brings,
The glad renewal of the earth that springs
To life with each resurgent season's roll—
The joyous resurrection of the soul.

We would pray for peace this Easter Day.
Let stones of hate and fear be rolled away,
That love, so long entombed in hearts of men
May rise and live to rule the world again.

Let hearts be opened wide this Easter time
That he, who made the sacrifice sublime
And rose from death's dark tomb to live alway,
May walk and talk with us this Easter Day.

That we may feel his presence by our side,
Our Master, Friend, our Teacher and our Guide;
That we may know he moves among us still,
Your living messenger of peace—good will.

Awaken each of us to our own worth
In making true his dream of peace on earth,
That this beloved world, so torn by strife,
May rise, with him, to new and glorious life.

# Co-Creators

I'm glad God leaves a part
Of his creation up to me;
I'm glad he puts a challenge here
And gives me eyes to see
The part that I must play—
The work my hands alone must do
To bring about this portion
Of creation, fresh and new.

I'm glad that he sees fit to use
My small and humble gifts
To channel through to others
A bit of that which lifts;
I'm glad he's made of me
An instrument that I might give
A helping hand that others
More abundantly might live.

I'm glad he merely plants the seed
Then leaves it up to me
To cultivate the finished deed
Of better things to be.
I'm glad, so glad, to have a share
In adding to the worth,
The beauty and the glory
Of creation here on earth.

# I'm Glad

I'm glad the great Creator
  Arranged for there to be
A bit of work left over
  For the likes of you and me.

I'm sure he could have finished things—
  For instance—made the bread,
But no—he chose to give us little
  Grains of wheat, instead.

I'm sure he could have planted houses
  With no strain nor fuss;
Instead, he planted trees and left
  The building up to us.

I think he wanted us to share
  That joy and sheer elation
That builders and creators know
  Who see their own creation.

# An Artist's Prayer

Dear God and Ruler of all time,
We, who roam the realm of rhyme,
The world of word and song and art,
Would seek thy presence in our heart.

Give us the power to open eyes
To beauty of the earth and skies;
To open ears that they might hear
The angel voices ringing clear.

Lay thy hand on our pen and brush
That we may, in life's busy rush,
Create a spiritual rest
That all may feel refreshed and blest.

We thank thee for these gifts of thine,
For every talent is divine.
Then give us wisdom, Lord, we pray,
And guide us all in thine own way.

# God Is a Gracious Landlord

God is a gracious landlord;
   His generosity
Is equalled only by his boundless
   Love for you and me.

Were we to list his many gifts
   Laid up to our account,
We could not write them fast enough,
   So quickly they would mount.

Then, would we list our gifts to him
   And those made in his name,
I wonder—could we view those lists
   Without a sense of shame?

God is a gracious landlord,
   His giving knows no dearth—
How great our privilege to be
   His stewards here on earth.

# A Heaven Below

Let there be goodness and beauty,
And let there be eyes to see
Hearts stilled to reverent quiet,
Knowing it all comes from thee.

All hushed before the beauty
Of a sunset's glorious sky;
Let there be soft and gentle things—
A mother's sweet lullaby.

Let there be light and loveliness,
And let there be ears to hear
The sigh of wind in the branches,
The bird song ringing clear.

Let there be truth and honor,
And let there be minds that know
That beauty, goodness, light and love
Make life a heaven below.

# A Heaven Every Day

What wondrous miracles abound
  In ordinary things,
And yet how casually we see
  And hear a world that sings.
A rosebud bursts its prison pod
  And fragrance fills the air—
The tender grasses break the sod
  And green is everywhere.

A daisy lifts its dazzling smile
  To blue skies high above—
A maiden plucks the petals off
  And dreams of her true love.
A baby takes a faltering step—
  A brave soul smiles through pain.
The summer dies—the white snow flies—
  And spring is born again.

A universe of miracles,
  So very commonplace
We take them all for granted
  And accept with careless grace.
With wistful eyes we visualize
  A heaven far away,
The while we stumble blindly through
  A heaven every day.

# Let There Be Light

Let there be light—there is enough
Of dark along life's way;
Let there be warmth and sunshine,
Let there be dawn and day.

Let there be little children,
Let there be kites on strings,
Clowns and monkeys, and birthday cakes,
And gardens with small growing things.

Let there be music and dancing,
Let there be moonlit skies,
Let there be youth and romancing—
Lovers with stars in their eyes.

Let there be woods in September,
Let there be lilacs in spring,
Bright winter days to remember—
Let there be songs to sing.

Let there be peace and forgiving
With faith in the Father above—
Let there be triumphant living—
Let there be light—and love!

# Glory Forever

What a grand old world we live in,
  Spite of all its wars and strife—
What a glorious adventure
  To the heart in love with life!

There's a glory in the sunrise
  Of each fresh new day begun,
A satisfying glory in
  A good day's work well done.

The glory of enchantment
  At the beautiful and fair,
A glorious awareness
  Of God's presence everywhere.

A gladness and a glory
  In each friendship, old and new,
A glowing loyalty and trust
  That keeps those friendships true.

A sweet and wondrous glory
  In the love of man and maid;
A deep and gentle glory—
  Facing newness unafraid.

A thrilling, tingling glory
  In the mysteries of earth;
An awesome, reverent glory
  In the miracle of birth.

A radiance and glory
  In each challenge met and won;
A dignity and glory
  When the race of life is run.

A splendid, shining glory
  Like an aura that surrounds
The world of him within whose heart
  The love of life abounds.

# Memorial Day

Our fathers sacrificed so much
  To bring us liberty,
And many gave their lives that we
  Might be strong and free.

We think of family, home, and friends,
  This great land of the free
Where we can worship as we choose,
  Be what we want to be.

How glad we are to be alive
  In such a glorious day;
How grateful for the strength to meet
  Each challenge on our way!

This is the time we try to voice
  All that's in our heart,
And surely God must know and bless
  This day we set apart.

# We Pray

Lord of the nations all, we pray;
A sick, bewildered world today,
Groping our way in darkness, we
Have need of light that we may see;
Have need of truth, that we may know
The right, the sure, safe way to go.

Lord of the nations all, we plead
Forgiveness in our hour of need.
So many weary miles we've trod
On paths that lead away from God—
So many manmade plans we've tried,
So many of our sons have died—
So many schemes to no account,
When just the Sermon on the Mount,
Had we but listened, would have spared
This suffering the world has shared.

Lord of the nations all, hold high
The light of truth against the sky.
Perhaps we are not yet too blind
The path of righteousness to find,
The power of love to understand—
And then, if you will take our hand
And guide us, lest we stray again,
We shall find rest and peace—

                                    Amen.

41

# Beyond the Trivial

Oh, the daily busyness
That robs life of its luster—
The littleness that causes us
To bicker and to bluster.
We build upon our little cares
And let our worries mount
Till we miss all the glory
Of the things that really count.

Oh, the smallness of our lives,
The shame that we should be
Content to fence ourselves away
From life's nobility;
Content to keep our eyes upon
Our own small plot of ground
When glorious adventure
Lies in waiting all around.

Oh, the satisfaction—
If we could only know—
Of stretching out beyond ourselves
And letting ourselves grow
Beyond our little fenced-in plot
Of triviality
To join that great adventure
Life on earth was meant to be.

# A Promise Made

Be careful what you promise God—
  He'll take you at your word.
You may forget the prayer you said
  Or think it wasn't heard,
But some day when the time is right
  The door will open wide
And, hardly knowing how or why,
  You'll find yourself inside.

You'll find yourself conforming
  To that promise that you made,
For God believes in promises—
  His own are always paid.
And he believes in you and has
  Respect for what you say—
So take care what you promise
  And be prepared to pay.

# Along the Way

We cannot all be ministers
And preach with learned phrase;
Nor can we all be soloists
With golden song of praise;
But we can live a sermon here
And we can live a song,
And neither song nor sermon
Need be either loud or long;
But quietly, in little things
We do from day to day—
Some simple, kindly deed,
Some word of comfort we may say—
And, even though we're unaware
That such has been our goal,
Somewhere along the way an angel
Writes, "He saved a soul!"

# Insight and Farsight

Prayer is a mirror wherein we see
Ourselves and our world within;
Our secret longings, dearest loves,
The bent we have to sin;
Our needs and daily blessings,
Our weaknesses, our strength,
Our own soul's honest measurement—
Its height and depth and length.

And prayer, too, is a window
That shows the world outside.
We sense the greatness of God's hand,
How high, how deep, how wide;
A window where we stand and watch
Our neighbors passing there
And ease their heavy burdens
As we lift them up in prayer.

A mirror and a window—
Both reveal in countless ways
The insight and the farsight
That are hers who truly prays.

# And Wait on Thee

We pray, "Lord, these things we desire."
And then expect them to transpire
At once. We cannot see the way
That God must work. We merely pray,
And, puzzled, fail to understand
Why every petty small demand
Is not fulfilled forthwith. We say,
"If it be true that God is there,
Why, then, does he not answer prayer?"
Oh, of so little faith are we!
So small we are, we cannot see
The farflung ways God shapes our ends.
Our small mind only comprehends
The very near for which we yearn.
Oh, that we all might better learn
More patience—faith—that we might be
Willing to wait, dear Lord, on thee!

# There Is a Strength

There is a strength
That comes through prayer,
A confidence, a power,
A quiet, deep, unflinching faith
To meet the trying hour.

There is a peace
That comes through prayer,
A calm serenity
To face whatever life may hold
With grace and dignity.

There is a joy
That comes through prayer,
A gladness of the soul,
A glorious sense of having been
Refreshed, renewed, made whole.

# The Sound of Laughter

God must receive so many solemn prayers,
I think that he must relish now and then
A chuckle one in joy of living shares—
The sound of laughter from his world of men.

For faith—real, honest faith's a joyous thing,
Not easily compressed in hardbound rules,
And heaven's not where angels fear to sing,
Nor laughter meant to be confined to fools.

And if, in midst of prayer's solemnities,
An errant thought strays off to meet a smile,
I think that God smiles, too, at what he sees—
And both are made the happier for the while.

# Prayer Is a Medley

Prayer is a mixture of words and of working,
Thinking and acting, and promises made;
Dreaming and daring—and caring and sharing,
And following through with those promises paid.

Prayer is a medley of saying and doing,
Trying, denying, repenting, rebirth;
An inward and outward look at our living,
A revaluation of power and worth.

Prayer is a mingling of feeling and knowing,
A giving of thanks, an awareness of need;
Seeing, believing—and groping and growing
Higher and wider than dogma or creed.

Prayer is a union of faith and of reason,
A quelling of doubts, a resurgence of hope.
Prayer is the symphonic whole of our being,
The heartbeat of life in its noblest scope.

# Simplicity of Prayer

Prayer is such a simple thing—
  God's chapel is our own—
Just slipping in to sit awhile
  In thought with God alone.

Just opening and entering
  The chapel of our heart,
To rest awhile and talk with God
  And be with him apart.

To pause awhile in quietness
  Within his gentle peace,
And know the comfort and the joy
  Of prayer's profound release.

No hard-bound rules, no laws surround
  Its time, or place, or way,
For prayer fits into any
  Little corner of the day.

And what a joy it is to know
 The comforting release
From life's small cares and worries
 In that quiet time of peace.

Prayer gives strength beyond ourselves
 So mighty is its power,
That it can lend a radiance
 To every waking hour.

A radiance blooms forth in life
 Like flowers from the sod,
For every single minute that
 We spend in prayer with God.

Yes, prayer is such a simple thing
 To meet our God each day,
That we may live secure, and know
 He guides us on our way.

# Prayer of Trust

Lord, let me not be guilty
   Of the arrogance to be
Anxious as to what tomorrow
   Has in store for me,
In vain conceit believing
   That I, and I alone,
Must find the hidden answers
   To that vast and dim unknown.

I will, instead, be trusting
   As a child; will put my hand
With simple, childlike faith in thine,
   Not try to understand,
But trusting in thy loving care
   I will enter each new day
In humble gratefulness to thee
   For showing me the way.

# Outreach of Prayer

A prayer is a way of lifting ourselves,
Of getting a higher look,
Of reaching our thoughts to wider views,
Like reading a broadening book.

Prayer is a way of opening doors
We never had seen before;
From self-centered thoughts to those
That bring the whole world in rapport.

Prayer is an exercise of the soul,
Extending, enlarging our sight
To see our own life becoming
A part of all love and all light.

# Living Prayer

Prayer has many forms, I think.
In ways, far more than words, we link
Our hearts and souls to God. Perhaps
By just simple deed man taps
That reservoir of strength. No need
For words—his prayer lies in his deed.

Contrition, adoration, love,
Devotion to his God above—
All praise, all glory, all thanksgiving,
Are manifest in daily living.
Words are as empty as the air
Unless we truly live our prayer.

# September Hills

Have you seen the hills in September—
The aspens dripping their gold?
It's a picture no artist has painted,
A beauty no poet has told.

You must see for yourself the splendor
The glory that fills and thrills—
The gold of the sun on the aspens,
September high in the hills.

To stand by the road in the silence,
And feel the divine presence there,
The touch of the master artist
So evident everywhere.

To sense how the summer in dying
Has rallied its finest parade
And exits with banners flying,
Triumphant and unafraid.

If you've not seen the hills in September,
You must—for you'll never behold
A lovelier sight to remember
Than aspens' shimmering gold.

# Thanks Giving

I tried—I tried so very hard to pray,
To thank God for this lovely, lovely day;
But, as I knelt, so many blessings grew,
It seemed as though my heart would burst in two
With thankfulness—so many blessings there
To crowd into just one small "Thank you" prayer;
But as my lips groped haltingly to find
The words to speak my humbly grateful mind,
I heard God's gentle whisper, kneeling there,
"Arise my child, your heart said your prayer."

# Thanksgiving Day

This is the time, the special time,
The day we set apart
To try to voice the gratitude
We feel deep in our heart.

The time when we become aware
Of blessings, great and small,
And realize we never can
Give proper thanks to all.

But since God understands and hears
The language of the heart,
I'm sure he knows and cherishes
This day we set apart.

# One Hushed Moment

For one hushed moment we see them there,
The three wise men with their treasures rare,
The lowly shepherds come to adore
The King they had so long waited for.
For one hushed moment—then lost to sight
In the deepening dark of time's long night;
But for that moment each in his way
Lives in the heart of man today.

For one hushed moment of time each year
Your heart and mine are given to hear
The angel chorus and see the star
Bidding us, too, come, travel afar;
Bidding us come out of doubt's dark night
Into the stable's holy light;
Bidding us follow the star's bright beams
Into the joy of remembered dreams.

For one hushed moment we sense the glory
The shepherds knew in the Christmas story,
And see, as the wise men saw above,
The radiant light of peace and love.
For one hushed moment in time's swift race,
We pause in wonder before his grace,
And life is richer and love more fair
For one hushed moment that we spend there.

# To God with Love

We've all known that special lift
Felt when we bestow a gift
On some dear one—a friend or kin.
Little card, "With love," tucked in.

There is no begrudging there—
Such a joy it is to share
Blessings that we have with others,
Friends and neighbors, sisters, brothers.

Such a happy way to say
That they're loved a special way;
Such a nice way to express
All our love and gratefulness.

So it is with gifts we bring
As our heart's thank-offering
Token of our gratitude
For the beautiful and good.

Symbol of our grateful praise
For his blessings all our days.
Thus, we give our Friend above
These, our gifts—"To God with love."

# In Gentleness and in Beauty

In the still of a winter's midnight,
   Christmas had its start,
In the soft, seeking cry of a baby boy
   Held to his mother's heart.

In the misty blue of a star's light,
   Christmas came to earth,
With the echo of angel voices
   Singing the Christ Child's birth.

In gentleness and in beauty
   This Christmastime we share
Came to perform its miracle
   On our hearts everywhere.

And still in the thoughtful quiet,
   In the midst of its merry joy,
The heart finds the meaning of Christmas
   In the gift of that baby boy.

# A Sprig of Brightness

As we come away from Christmas
  To our old routine again
Let us work a little harder
Toward goodwill among all men.

Let us strengthen our resolve to use
  A little more restraint,
A little more compassion, and
  A little less complaint.

A deeper understanding
  And a great deal more of giving;
A bit more concentration
  On the finer side of living.

As we take down the Christmas tree
  And store the wreath away,
Let's keep a sprig of brightness
  To remind us of this day.

One little sprig of brightness
  To help us to remember
That love and cheer are not confined
  To one day in December.

# My Church Home

This is my home, my church home,
  The place where I belong,
Where friends and loved ones join with me
  In praise and prayer and song.

This is my home, my church home,
  With doors that open wide,
Where I can come when cares beset
  And know love waits inside.

This is my home, my church home,
  My haven from the storm,
Where friendly hands reach out to me,
  Gracious and true and warm.

This is my home, my church home—
  Oh, would that I could share
Its strength and love and peace and joy
  With all folk everywhere.

# The Living Church

This, then, is the church—not brick nor stone,
Nor leaded pane, nor heaven-pointed spire.
If we would see the real church we must look
Fathoms deeper, infinitely higher,
Beyond the narrow borders of our sight,
For boundless and eternal is its scope—
Wide as the very love of God is wide,
As deep as faith, unquenchable as hope.

Within the hearts and lives of those who've known
Its healing touch, its power to remold,
It walks the streets of life, a living thing,
To challenge and inspire young and old.
Through you and me, and Christians everywhere,
The living church moves on, an endless chain—
The touch of life on life—a heritage
Of riches deepening with every strain.

No stationary monument is this,
For, be it humble room or work of art,
The church is only real as it becomes
God's gift of love passed on from heart to heart.

# As We Go

And now we ask God's blessing
As we go our separate ways;
May he walk beside and guide us
In the living of our days.

May he heighten our awareness
Of the good and true and fine,
And kindle humble gratitude
Within your heart and mine.

May he give our faith a substance
That the world can see and feel,
And may we put that faith to work
With love-inspired zeal.

May our trust in him be strengthened
By each trial along the way,
As we go now with his blessing,
In whose blessed name we pray.